WHAT'S MONEY ALL ABOUT?

BY LAURA CRAWFORD

PEARSON

Scott
Foresman

Editorial Offices: Glenview, Illinois • Parsippany, New Jersey • New York, New York
Sales Offices: Needham, Massachusetts • Duluth, Georgia • Glenview, Illinois
Coppell, Texas • Ontario, California • Mesa, Arizona

TABLE OF CONTENTS

Chapter 1 *A World of Money*

What did people do before there was money? How were they paid for their work? Before money, how did humans get what they needed to survive?

Thousands of years ago, there was no such thing as money. As time passed, people found it was useful for doing business. Today, each country has a form of money, or **currency.** The currency of the United States is the dollar. Mexico uses pesos. The English have used pounds for hundreds of years, while most of Europe now uses the euro. The currency in China is the renminbi, and the yen is used in Japan.

Stock exchange in Hong Kong, China

As you know, people use money to buy goods and services. People also store their money in banks. But did you know that every day, different currencies are traded for one another?

Imagine that you are going to leave the United States to visit London, England. When you arrive in London you will need English money to buy food, ride on a bus, or visit a museum. In London, or even before you leave the United States, you can trade in United States dollars for English pounds.

There's much more that we could discuss about modern currency. But let's first rewind to the start of human civilization. Let's look at how trading, buying, and selling used to work.

Chapter 2 *Bartering*

Long before there was modern money, people had ways to get food and supplies. People would grow, catch, or make most things. Then they would barter, or trade, for things that they couldn't grow, catch, or make.

Some people focused on farming, growing as much food as they could. Other people concentrated on fishing or hunting, catching as many fish and land animals as they could. Others were skilled craftsmen. Through bartering, many people were able to share the crops raised by the farmers, the fish caught by the fishermen, the animals caught by the hunters, and the goods made by the craftsmen.

Bartering was not always easy. Often people could not agree on the value of the items they wanted to trade.

An argument might have arisen between a fisherman and a hunter trying to barter with each other. The fisherman may have thought that one deer was worth five fish, and the hunter may have thought the deer was worth one hundred fish.

People often had to **compromise,** or give up some of their demands, so an agreement could be made. Think about the fisherman and the hunter. To compromise, the fisherman may have given the hunter sixty fish in exchange for his deer.

When two people discuss, or sometimes argue over, a price, it is called **bargaining.** Both the fisherman and the hunter would have wanted and needed as much food as possible. They would have bargained until each felt the trade was fair.

Egyptians trading goods

Some of the earliest evidence of goods being bartered are found in ancient Egyptian paintings. Some of the paintings show people exchanging bread for fish. They also show wooden boxes being traded for shoes.

The Egyptians bartered with each other, but they also bartered with other countries. The Egyptians sent stones, copper, grain, and papyrus to the people who lived in ancient Lebanon. In exchange, the Egyptians received wood such as fir, cedar, and pine. Through bartering, both the Egyptians and the people of ancient Lebanon got things that could not be found in their home countries.

Bartering and bargaining took place all over the world. In parts of coastal Africa, people spoke many languages. Sometimes, two groups of people wanted to barter but could not communicate. So what did they do? They used "silent trading" when dealing with each other. Here's how silent trading worked: Traveling traders would call out, alerting local traders that they had arrived and were ready to trade.

Outdoor market in Mali, Africa

Silk cloth from China

The traveling traders would then leave spices, jewels, minerals, precious stones, or horses on a beach. They would wait for the local people to come and look at the goods. The local traders would then leave wood, cloth, fine metalwork, glass, or dried fish on the beach. Each group returned and decided if the trade was fair. If either group didn't like the goods being offered, it would not take them. The groups returned with different items until everyone was satisfied. The entire trade was done without any speaking. Sometimes the traders never even saw each other!

Chapter 3 *Forms of Money*

Bartering goods and services did not always work, so people began using items as money. One important form of early money was salt. For thousands of years in Africa and Asia, salt was used for money. That is where we get the word "salary!" Salary means the amount of money that a person is paid for work. There were many reasons to use salt as money. It was easy to measure and easy to carry. In some ancient lands, salt was more precious than gold!

Modern Ethiopian women and children load a donkey with bags of salt for trade.

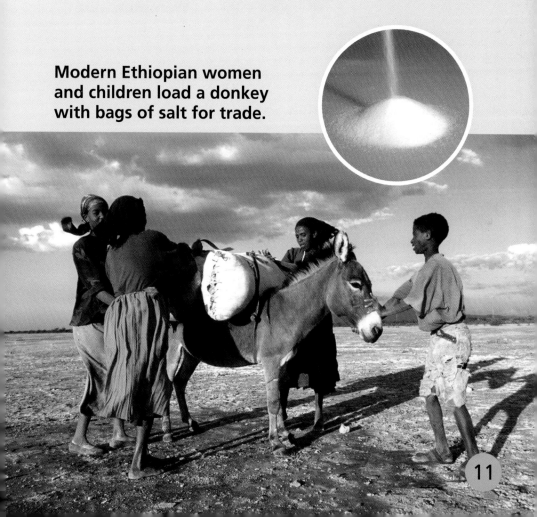

Wampum belt

In North America, Native Americans used **wampum** for trading and ceremonial purposes. The Native Americans polished white and purple shells. They strung the shells like beads in patterns, making wampum belts or necklaces. One black bead might be worth several white beads, and one belt could contain as many as 360 beads. The wampum system worked well for Native Americans when they were trading with each other. However, it was difficult for them to trade with people who thought that wampum had little value.

It was hard for people to agree on the value of things like salt and wampum. More people worldwide were trading, or doing business, with each other. They traded within their communities and traveled to other countries to trade. It was even harder to agree on how much things were worth from country to country.

People established coin-based systems of money. Coins were decided upon for a good reason: They can be small and easy to carry! Historians think that the first coins were used about three thousand years ago, although they are unsure of the exact date.

Ancient trade ship

In what is now the country of Turkey, coins made of silver and gold were stamped with a value. This idea spread to Europe and then to other parts of the world. With the coin's value stamped on its surface, people could figure out how much to charge for their goods.

Shekel from the Roman period

Chapter 4 *Money for the United States*

During colonial times, the colonies used British pounds. This turned into a big problem when the colonies became the United States of America. The new country needed its own money.

The answer to the problem was to create a system of coin-based money that the entire country could use. In 1792 Congress authorized coins that all thirteen states could use for trade. Our country's earliest coins were small and round, with thirteen interlocking rings around the edges. One side of the coin said, "WE ARE ONE," while the other said, "MIND YOUR BUSINESS."

Early American coin

Today our coins are made in four **mints** located around the country. When you look at a coin, you can see markings on it. If you see the letter D on an American coin, it tells you that the coin was minted, or made, at the mint in Denver, Colorado. If you spot the letter P on a coin, it means that the coin was minted in Philadelphia, Pennsylvania. The other mints (in San Francisco, California, and West Point, New York) make coins for coin collectors. Therefore, the coins that you use in the marketplace have either a D or a P stamped on them.

Our dollar bills are printed at the Bureau of Engraving and Printing in Washington, D.C. They are printed on large sheets of paper made with linen and cotton. Special ink is used to create the images and writing on each bill.

American dollar bills are just one form of modern currency. People all over the world use money to get what they need. From salt to coins, money keeps changing. Who knows what we'll use as money in the future!

Stacks of American one dollar bills lined up in a machine at the Bureau of Printing and Engraving in Washington, D.C.

Now Try This

The United States Mint

There are hundreds of resources available for people who are interested in news about money. However, when it comes to United States currency, there is one source that you should check first: the official Web site of the United States Mint. Using a computer, type the words "United States Mint" into a search engine. One of the first Web addresses you will see will be the official Web site of the United States Mint.

Once you are on the site, start exploring! One of the first things you will notice is that the Department of the Treasury oversees the United States Mint. There are many more interesting facts to be found at the United States Mint Web site.

Get together in small groups and carefully look over the contents of the United States Mint Web site. Then assign each group member one section of the site to research. When each group member has finished researching, meet again to share your information.

Here are some questions to help guide you in doing your research and presenting your information: What section of the site did you research? What did you find out? What more would you like to know about what you researched? Did the Web site lead you to any other Web sites? What questions were answered by your research? Do you have more questions?

19

Glossary

bargaining *n.* working together to come up with an agreement on a price.

compromise *v.* to give up some of your original demands in order to reach an agreement with someone.

currency *n.* any kind of money used as a medium of exchange.

mints *n.* places where money is coined by the government.

wampum *n.* beads made from shells, formerly used by Native Americans as money.